Little
Cauldron
of
Love Spells

Little Cauldron of Love Spells

Midia Star

A GODSFIELD BOOK
www.godsfieldpress.com

This book is dedicated to every woman
who needs a little love in her life.

First published in Great Britain in 2004
by Godsfield Press, a division of
Octopus Publishing Group Ltd
2–4 Heron Quays
Docklands
London E14 4JP

10 9 8 7 6 5 4 3 2 1

Printed and bound in China

ISBN 1 84181 238 2
EAN 9781841812380

Disclaimer
This book is intended to give general information
only. The publisher, author and distributor expressly
disclaim all liability to any person arising directly or
indirectly from the use of, or any errors or omissions
in, the information in this book. The adoption and
application of the information in this book is at the
reader's discretion and is their sole responsibility.

Contents

Introduction

Welcome to this book, which is designed so that you can dip into it whenever you feel the need for a little magick in your life. When you have a problem in your love life, pick up this little cauldron of love spells and you will find the answer – a girl should never be without it!

This is a collection of romantic magick spells and charms guaranteed to help you find true love or mend a broken heart. I have selected all the spells so that anyone can use this book – there are no expensive ingredients to buy or complicated rituals to perform, and you don't need to be a fully fledged witch in order to create a bit of magick in your love life.

The book is divided into two sections. The first is dedicated to finding love and keeping love alive, including:

- Attracting a suitable partner
- Finding a soulmate

- Keeping your true love interested
- Having a successful marriage.

The second section is designed for those times when things aren't quite going to plan in the love department; it includes spells and charms for:

- Stopping arguments
- Making up after a break-up
- Banishing an unsuitable partner
- Getting over a break-up.

All the spells and charms in this book have been tried and tested and have been personally selected by me. You do not need any special items – no blood of bat or eye of newt required! All that is needed with every spell or charm is your belief that it will work. I hope you enjoy working with this little cauldron of spells and bringing the magick back into your love life.

The rules of The Craft

I like to include a small amount of information about spell craftwork in my books. Although I have no intention of preaching to you, it is important to know a few 'house rules' when working with magick. If you try to perform spells without any knowledge of how spell crafting works, your spells will either fail to work or will have disastrous consequences. Here are some rules that you should take note of when you apply practical magick to your love life.

You can't force someone to love you!

No matter how hard you try, you cannot make someone fall in love with you if they aren't the least bit interested – and to try will only cause you harm. The power of magick has the ability to suggest and make it known that you are interested in a particular person. But it won't perform miracles or make someone who isn't interested fall in love with you. You should never, ever try to influence another person's thoughts, no matter how much you think it will benefit them. Thankfully, we all have our own minds, but trying to control another person's mind will only result in a great deal of unhappiness.

The Threefold Law

Different magick books give different 'rules', but every book you read about spell craft will tell you about the Threefold Law. This is the most important rule that you will learn and is not solely applicable to witches – it is the way of the universe. You've doubtless heard the saying 'Luck comes in threes'. Well, there is truth in this saying – whatever you give

out comes back to you three times. In fact, it can come back to you up to seven times! If you do something that is regarded as unpleasant to another person or living thing, then it will come back to you at some point in your life, and never as you would have imagined. The same applies if you do something beneficial to another person.

Your true intention counts

Please don't panic after reading about the Threefold Law and think that because you accidentally kicked the cat this morning, you will be 'paid back'! Accidental occurrences don't count. It's your true intention that is important. If you intentionally spread malicious gossip about someone, then at some point in your life you will suffer because of it. But if you accidentally do something to harm someone, don't panic – if you genuinely didn't mean to, then all will be fine.

Whoops – I've made a mistake!

Love spells are the most powerful spells you can perform because they deal with one of the deepest emotional feelings that we have. If you perform a spell and later regret doing it, don't worry. As I mentioned earlier, it's your *true* intention that counts, and if you performed a spell because someone else suggested that you do it, it wouldn't work anyway. It's got to be *your* desire. If you do a spell and then decide it was not such a good idea after all, you can always retract it – I'll show you how to do this in the Conclusion (see pages 124–125).

Tools of the trade

This is a topic that receives a lot of debate where spell crafters are concerned. Some books will blind you with what I call 'witchy babble', telling you that you *must* have a wand; an altar; a selection of herbs (which are often hard to obtain); a pentagram engraved in the middle of your bedroom; plus all manner of paraphernalia, if you are to perform 'real' magick. This is not entirely true. I've often been in a situation where I've had no tools available and yet have performed a successful spell just by using the power of belief. Many people can't afford all the gadgets that are available to perform practical magick, and others wish to keep their interest in magick quiet from family and friends – and a massive pentagram and an altar in your bedroom would soon have tongues wagging!

If you really want to buy some of the 'tools of the trade', then by all means go ahead, but it is not a necessary part of spell work. Years before the invention of New Age shops, witches had to rely on what was readily available from nature to enhance their spells – and the best thing is that all the herbs and natural products that help a spell to be more effective are free! So if you've been blinded by witchy babble before, forget it – you don't *need* it.

The power of the moon

Because the moon has a great influence on our lives as a whole, I have included a small amount of information regarding it, and how it can enhance your spells at certain times of the month. It isn't imperative that you do a spell on a certain moon phase. If, for example, you wanted to attract a loving partner into your life and the moon was in a banishing phase, you could simply turn the spell around so that you stated that you wanted to banish loneliness from your love life. The moon has eight phases per 28 days.

• The new (or dark) moon – when the moon is not visible in the sky

• The first waxing crescent – when the moon is a slim D-shape

• The first quarter – when it looks like a half-moon in a D-shape

• The waxing gibbous moon – when the moon is a slim oval shape

• The full moon – when the moon looks like a bright, round ball

• The waning gibbous moon – when it is a slim oval shape

• The last quarter – when the moon looks like a half-moon in a C-shape

• The first waning crescent – when the moon is a slim C-shape.

The easiest way to remember your magick-making moon rules is that if you want something positive to happen, you will give it more power by doing the spell on a full or waxing moon. If you wish something to disappear from your life, you should do the spell on a new (dark) or waning moon. So, if you want to attract a loving man into your life, you should do one of the attraction spells during a full or waxing (D-shaped) moon. If, on the other hand, you want to send a horrible man back where he belongs, you should do a banishing spell during a new or waning (C-shaped) moon.

The power of fire

Candles represent the fire element in our world and play an important part in spell crafting.

It is believed that specific days and certain coloured candles can enhance a spell, speeding it up and making it more powerful.

Try to use the following candles for your love spells:

• A pink or a red candle for increasing love.

• A blue or black candle for decreasing and banishing love.

If you can't find the correct colour of candle for a particular spell, you can always use a normal white household candle, which is easy to obtain from any store or supermarket.

The best days for relationship magick are:

• Tuesday – spells for protection and banishing

• Friday – spells for attraction

• Saturday – spells for banishing

• Sunday – spells for confidence and success

However, it isn't essential that you do a certain spell on a certain day, with a particular coloured candle, under a specific moon phase. The wonderful thing about magick is that you can do it at any time. So long as you believe in it and respect it, it will work just as well – maybe not as fast, but it will still work for you.

Looking-for-love spells

This section is all about finding love and keeping it alive. When performing a spell for love, you need to be specific as to what you want – but not so explicit as to target a particular person. Everyone is entitled to his or her own free will, and if the man you've got your eye on isn't remotely interested in you, trying to bewitch him is a dangerous game and will only result in heartache for you. So be warned!

By 'specific' I mean stating what kind of man you want to share your life with. Would you like someone who is older than you? Younger than you? The same age as you? Do you prefer someone who is average-looking, but with whom you can have an intelligent conversation? Or maybe you prefer someone who resembles a model and who will cook you dinner every night and do the washing up, without complaining that it's not his turn – yes, I know that's asking for the impossible, but you never know!

Before you cast a spell, think carefully about what it is that you really want (and, more importantly, what you don't want) in your love life. If you simply ask for lots of love and to be wanted and needed, you might find six adorable kittens on your doorstep!

Remember: be specific! If you forget to mention a few things, you may well end up with someone who is completely unsuitable for you.

Paper love

What better way to find your ideal man than to design him yourself! This is a traditional Romany spell with a modern touch.

You will need

One sheet of pink letter paper

Scissors

A pen

Sticky tape or glue

Four drops of rose oil

What you do

Do this spell on a Friday night.

Fold the piece of paper in two and cut it in half. On one half draw the figure of a man – just as if you were drawing 'paper people'.

Take your pen and write on him all the positive attributes you require in your ideal man. These might be: kind, caring, good looking, wears spectacles, and so on. Everything you desire you should write down on him. Next draw a picture of a woman on the other piece of paper. This represents you, so you need to think positively and write down all your good points on the paper lady. You could put something like: I am confident, fun to be with, kind-

hearted, an excellent host, interesting to talk to, and so on.

Now that you have the perfect couple, you need to cut them out and join their hands together so that they look as though they are holding hands. Use some sticky tape or glue to do this. Then pour two drops of rose oil onto each figure and say:

This man represents you
This woman represents me.
Goddess, find my ideal man
And send him on to me
So mote it be.

Leave your paper couple on the bedroom windowsill for 28 days.

Personal ad

This spell is designed to attract love to you by way of sending a personal advertisement into the universe. Don't worry, for no one else will see this spell, so you can really let your imagination go wild and write down everything you want in your ideal man.

You will need

A word processor or PC

Paper to print on

Scissors

One pink candle

Matches or a lighter

What you do

Do this spell on a full moon.

You've doubtless seen the personal ads at the back of newspapers and magazines. You are now going to design your own personal ad to send out to the universe – but don't panic, you are not required actually to send this to a newspaper or magazine, so you can be as specific as you like!

Type out your 'wanted' ad on your word processor or PC and print it onto a sheet of paper. It might read something like this:

Wanted!
A Prince Charming
required to
Sweep this princess off
her feet.
Must be kind,
considerate and
Make her feel like
a million dollars.
Only genuine princes
need apply.

Cut out your advert and place it under your pink candle. Light the candle. You can now sit back and relax. Let the universe take care of the rest and carry your wish to all those available bachelors!

I want that man

This spell is designed to attract an ideal man to you using the ingredients listed below, to ensure he is everything you need in a partner.

You will need

One large horse-chestnut leaf (for strength)

One ball of cotton wool (for softness)

One hard-boiled sweet (tough on the outside, sweet on the inside)

One white feather (for kindness)

A piece of string

What you do

Do this spell on a Friday night and a full moon.

Find a quiet moment when you can relax in a nice warm bath. Place the horse-chestnut leaf in the bath water with you and, while you relax, imagine what your ideal man will be like. Your visualization energies will be transported to the leaf.

When you get out of the bath, wrap yourself in a big fluffy towelling robe or towel. Lay the leaf on a hard surface (such as a dressing table) and place the cotton-wool ball, the boiled sweet and the feather in the middle of the leaf. Fold the sides of the leaf up to the centre and tie your parcel with the string. Say, 'I want that man!'

Bury the parcel in the front of your garden or in a windowbox at the front of your house or apartment and wait for the magick to take effect.

Attracting commitment

You may have no problem attracting men, but there comes a time in every woman's life when she wants a bit of commitment from a man – even if it's just introducing you to his mother. This spell will attract only men who are true to you and who will commit to you.

You will need

A strip of paper

A tall glass of orange juice

A handful of seasonal berries (strawberries, raspberries, and so on)

One drop of rose oil

A blender

A romantic novel

What you do

Do this spell on a waxing moon.

Write the following words on the strip of paper:

> *This man I meet will*
> *never stray*
> *This man I meet won't*
> *run away*
> *This man I meet will*
> *be Mr Perfect*
> *This man I meet*
> *will want to commit*
> *So mote it be.*

Pour the orange juice, berries and rose oil into the blender, and blend for one minute. Pour the mixture into the tall glass. Dip the strip of paper into the glass and allow it to soak up some of the juice.

Take it out again and place the strip on a sunny windowsill to dry. Drink your glass of juice. When the paper is dry, place it between the pages of your favourite romantic novel and wait for Mr Commitment to come into your life.

An irresistible charm

This charm is designed to attract the opposite sex to you. Friday is the day devoted to Venus, the goddess of love, so do this spell on a Friday night if you can. You will soon be surprised by how many men you attract. You might even have to fight them off!

You will need

A handful of dried lavender

Six dried rose petals

A pinch of rose talcum powder

A pinch of red glitter

A small bowl

A small purse

What you do

Do this spell on a Friday night.

This simple charm is easy to perform and takes a matter of minutes. Mix all the ingredients together in a small bowl. Play some of your favourite music while you do this and then close your eyes and say the following words:

Attractive to the opposite sex I will be
Tonight they will flock to me.
The pick of the best will come to me
This is my wish, so mote it be.

Pour the mixture into your purse and place it in your bag. Take the purse with you when you go out for the evening and see just how many men can't resist you!

Magick clay man

We all aspire to have the ideal man in our lives and, when your heart has been broken in too many pieces to count, you begin to wish you could design your very own perfect man. Well, now you can!

You will need

A large piece of air-drying modelling clay

One teaspoon of dried lavender

A selection of buttons

A small piece of red or pink ribbon

What you do

Make your clay man on a Sunday, the day of creativity.

Before you begin modelling your clay man, knead the clay so that it becomes pliable and soft. When you are almost ready, take the teaspoon of dried lavender and sprinkle it into the clay, then knead it again so that the dried lavender gets mixed up in the clay.

Now you can start shaping your clay man. Where you begin is entirely up to you, and you don't need to be a trained sculptor to create your model – the most important thing is that you make it yourself.

When you feel happy with his shape, you can begin to decorate him. Add buttons for the eyes and nose, etch a nice smile on his face and put some more buttons where his shirt would be. When you are satisfied with the way he looks, tie a small piece of red or pink ribbon round his neck. When he is dry (this usually takes about 24 hours), whisper to him to find your ideal man. You should meet him very soon.

27

Fake it and make it spell

This is the simplest of spells you can do, but it does require a lot of visualization.

You will need

Somewhere quiet where you can relax for half an hour

What you do

You can do this spell any time and anywhere.

Close your eyes and imagine there's a big white cinema screen in front of you. On the cinema screen, place images of any negative thoughts you have about yourself. You might think you're not pretty enough to attract a man, or you're too tall, too short, too fat, too thin, have a big bottom.

Now imagine that you have a big red marker pen in your hand. Scribble each negative image out with the pen, so that you can no longer see them.

Now the cinema screen is completely white again and you are going to place only positive images on it. Put anything and everything that you desire to be true on this new screen. If you wish you were taller, shorter, fatter or thinner, then place the image of the 'new you' on your screen. This in turn will be the way you portray yourself to others in the future.

If you do this ritual for two weeks, you will notice that your confidence and self-worth will soar – and others will notice it, too!

Keeping him interested

Keeping a relationship alive can be hard work. If you have family commitments, children or you have to work, then your love life can quickly be demoted to the 'not-so-important' pile of things to do. If you think your man is losing interest in you, try this candle spell from Holland.

You will need

One tall white candle

One tall pink candle

A piece of white cotton thread

A piece of pink cotton thread

Two drops of rose oil

A flower pot with some soil in it

Matches or a lighter

What you do

This love spell is best done on Midsummer's Night (24 June), but can also be performed on a Friday.

Take your two candles and bind them together with the two pieces of coloured thread. Sprinkle two drops of rose oil onto the candles, then place them in the flower pot of soil. At midnight, light the two candles and say the following three times:

These two candles bind our love
Send this wish to the sky above
May he always stay interested in me
So mote it be.

Allow the candles to burn down until there is 2.5cm (1in) left, then blow them out. When the wax is cool, take the candles out of the flower pot and bury the candle stubs in the soil. It is important that you leave this outside for 14 days.

Spicy sex life

If you want to spice up your sex life, try making this delicious fruity drink for the two of you to share. If you don't drink alcohol, you can do this spell using a bottle of fruit juice or non-alcoholic wine (readily available from most grocery stores).

You will need

One bottle of red wine

A large saucepan

Three drops of lemon oil

Three tablespoons of sugar

Five blackberries

Three drops of vanilla essence

A piece of muslin or a clean tea-towel

A large jug

One pink candle

Matches or a lighter

What you do

You can do this spell on any night of the week.

Pour the bottle of red wine into the saucepan. Add the lemon oil, sugar, blackberries and vanilla essence. Gently heat the mixture on the stove and allow the ingredients to combine together. Allow the mixture to cool and then drain it through a piece of muslin or a clean tea-towel into a large jug.

When your love arrives, pour the mixture back into the bottle and light the pink candle. Pour three glasses of magick wine – one for yourself, one for your partner and one for the goddess of love. Say the following just once:

This wine I drink with you tonight
Our desire and passion will soon ignite.

Relax and enjoy your evening together – it should be one to remember!

To find the perfect love

Wouldn't it be great to do a spell and discover you have found the perfect partner? Well, this spell will help you find the ideal man for you. Remember to be specific about what it is – and isn't – that you seek in a partner!

You will need

A small piece of paper

A pen

One white envelope

Five pink rose petals

One red candle

Matches or a lighter

A heatproof dish

What you do

Do this spell on a waxing moon.

Take the piece of paper and write on it the following words:

I wish to find my perfect partner
Carry this message over land and water.
Take my wish for all to see
Allow my soulmate to come to me.

Place the piece of paper into your envelope and seal it. Arrange the five rose petals round the red candle and light it. Place the envelope behind the candle while it burns. When it has burned halfway down, light one corner of the envelope and drop it into the heatproof dish. Allow the flames to engulf the envelope.

When you are left with ash, take it outside and bury it in your garden. Your wish will be carried all round the world and your Mr Perfect will soon make himself known to you.

Getting over a break-up

Breaking up is hard to get over at the best of times, but if you allow yourself to wallow in brooding over it, you prevent yourself from meeting your *true* destiny. This little spell will help you get over the heartache. The spell is cast in two stages. The first stage is to banish your heartache, and the second is to send a message to every bachelor out there that you are raring to go again.

You will need

One dark blue candle and candle holder

A handful of salt

Matches or a lighter

One pink candle

One crystal

What you do

Do this spell on a Saturday when the moon is waning.

Take the blue candle and place it on your windowsill in the candle holder. Cup the salt in your hand and pour a circle of it all round the candle. Light the candle, close your eyes and say:

*The heartache I feel must go away
It does me no good to feel this way.
Take my heartache and set me free
So that I can find love again and be happy.*

Allow the candle to burn down. Wait two hours, then take the pink candle and place it in the same candle holder. Put the crystal in front of the pink candle, then light the candle. Say:

*I am now free to find love again
Send this message to the universe
So that I may find true love
And keep true love.*

Allow the pink candle to burn down completely, and place the crystal in your purse or handbag.

A marriage made in heaven

If you are attending a wedding and are stuck for a gift, or if you are getting married yourself, make this easy charm for wedded bliss for whoever is getting married.

You will need

12 large leaves (of any kind)

One red rose

A few lavender flowers

A pinch of thyme

A pinch of rosemary

A pinch of mixed spice

A red ribbon

What you do

You should do this spell on the night before the wedding.

Arrange the leaves to make a bed of leaves, then lay the rose on top in the centre. Sprinkle the lavender flowers, thyme, rosemary and mixed spice onto the rose. Wrap the leaves and their contents round the rose stem, then tie it all up with the red ribbon, saying:

*This rose represents a blessed marriage
With nothing but happiness, love and joy
May this marriage last for evermore.*

If this is a gift for another couple, place the rose in a vase and give it to the bride. If it is for your own wedding, carry the rose in your bouquet of flowers on your wedding day. You can dry the rose out and it will be a keepsake for evermore.

Engaging Times

It can be a bit daunting announcing to the world that you
intend to spend the rest of your life with your current partner,
and you may still have worries that the two of you are
doing the right thing. If you've recently got engaged and
want to ensure that you are both committed to one another,
try this spell.

You will need

A bowl of water

Your engagement ring

Nine rose petals

One rose quartz crystal

1m (1yd) pink ribbon

What you do

Do this spell on a Friday.

This spell will make sure that your engagement is full of happy times together, whether you have a long engagement or a short one. First of all, fill the bowl with water and then add your engagement ring. Next add the rose petals, the rose quartz and finally the pink ribbon. Hold both your hands over the bowl and repeat the following nine times:

*By the power created
by Venus
Goddess of love
I call upon you
Up above*

*To bring me only
happy times
With the person that I
have in mind.*

Swirl your left hand around in the water for a moment. You should feel that it has become warm and soothing. Leave the bowl with its contents overnight.

The following morning, take your engagement ring, the rose quartz and the pink ribbon out of the bowl, then leave the bowl of water outside for the birds to drink. Until you marry, sleep with the rose quartz under your pillow and carry the ribbon with you wherever you go.

Irresistible and kissable

We all like to look good when we go out, don't we? This little
beauty spell is not only easy to do, but is designed so that
you will look irresistible and kissable when you head out for
the evening. How many kisses will you get tonight?

You will need

One drop of vanilla essence

Your best lipstick

What you do

Do this spell on a full moon.

Rub the vanilla essence over the shaft of the lipstick and allow it to dry. Just before you are due to go out, carefully apply your lipstick and visualize its being your ultimate attraction weapon. Smack your lips together and say:

My lips are so kissable
They will make me
irresistible
Men will not be able
to resist
The power of my kiss.

Now go out and knock 'em dead! I'm sure this spell was designed for Cinderella, because it only lasts for one night. But you can refresh it by repeating the ritual whenever you need it. If, like most women, you have a variety of lipsticks that you wear for different occasions, you can simply repeat the spell whenever you use a different shade.

Love superstitions

Years ago people believed in all manner of superstitions, including various do's and don'ts for matters of the heart. Here are just a few that I have unearthed:

Traditionally 14 February was the day when birds chose their mates. If you see any of the following birds on St Valentine's Day, it reveals something about your future love life:

Blackbird – signifies the clergy, so a possible wedding is in store for you
Red-breasted bird – tells of a sailor who will fall in love with you
Goldfinch – prophesies a millionaire who is close by and fond of you
Yellow bird – foretells a life of riches
Sparrow – this humble bird signifies a love cottage
Bluebird – unfortunately, this bird foretells poverty
Dove – always foretells good luck and fortunate times ahead.

Are you thinking about getting married in June? If you are, then according to an ancient Roman proverb:

Prosperity to the man and happiness to the maid who marry in June.

If a girl meets her sweetheart or kisses him for the first time under the light of the moon it is considered to be lucky for the couple.

If you are thinking about a man you like and you hear a cockerel crow, you will marry him.

If you fall up the stairs you will soon hear of a wedding.

When working with the one you love, it is lucky if you meet a black cat or a white horse.

You should announce an engagement on a Saturday and offer marriage on a Friday.

Love me, love my children

Marriages and partnerships don't always last for ever and sometimes we find ourselves free to look for a new partner after divorce or separation. Often that means that we already have children from a previous partnership. For a new man to come into your life, he will have to accept and love your children as much as he loves you. This spell comes from passionate Italy and will ensure that your new man will love and respect your children as much as you do.

You will need

One red candle

A child's toy

One red feather

One white feather

One bay leaf

Matches or a lighter

What you do

Do this spell on a new (dark) moon.

Place the red candle on a table where it won't be disturbed, and put the child's toy in front of it. Next place the red feather on one side of the candle and the white feather on the other side. Place the bay leaf behind the candle. Light the candle and visualize a happy and harmonious glowing red circle all round you. Say the following once:

To love me, you must also love all in my life
For me to love you, you must also love mine

This is my wish that you must obey
Otherwise I won't allow you to take my heart away
So mote it be.

Allow the candle to burn down. Take the feathers, bay leaf and any remaining candle wax and bury them in the garden of your home where your children play. This spell will make sure that whoever comes into your life looking for your love will accept that he has to love everything about you, including your children.

Find me Mr Right

There can come a time when you wonder if you're destined to spend a lifetime picking Mr Wrongs. This easy-to-make love charm comes from India and wards off unsuitable suitors, attracting Mr Right instead.

You will need

One black or grey pebble

A river

One white pebble

30cm (12in) length of leather thong

What you do

Do this spell on a full moon.

Depending on whether you are right- or left-handed, hold the black or grey pebble in your less dominant hand and visualize all the unsuitable men who have been in your life being absorbed into the pebble. Think about the traits they had that were unsuitable, and transfer these thoughts to the pebble. When you feel satisfied, open your hand and say:

Pebble, please take these unsuitable people out of my life and stop me from attracting them once and for all.

Now take the black or grey pebble to a river and toss it over your shoulder into the flowing water – don't look back at it.

When you get home, take the white pebble in your more dominant hand and visualize all the traits you would like to see in your Mr Right. Think carefully about what it is that you require from a partner, and again transfer all the energy into the white pebble. When you feel satisfied, take the piece of leather thong and wrap it round the pebble as many times as it will allow, tying it in a knot at the end. Keep this charm with you at all times for at least 28 days. You will stop attracting Mr Wrongs and will attract a suitable Mr Right instead.

Finding a soulmate

There are many nice, suitable men out there, but ultimately we all look for and need a soulmate to share our lives. It's all very well having a handsome young man on your arm, but if you have nothing in common, the novelty will soon wear off. This spell will seek out your very own soulmate.

You will need

12 pink rose petals

One pink candle

Matches or a lighter

One small seashell

What you do

Do this spell on a waxing moon.

Place the rose petals in a circle round the pink candle. Light the candle, then take the seashell and pass it through the candle flame five times – being very careful not to burn your fingers! As you do this, say:

By the power invested in me
I send you out to look for
my soulmate.
Bring him back to me
So that we can become one
So mote it be.

Allow the candle to burn down. Pick up the rose petals and throw them out of the window and into the universe. Imagine the wind taking the petals with your love message across the world. Carry your special shell with you and soon you will not only attract love, but will also meet your soulmate.

Reunion spell

Sometimes we lose touch with someone whom we realize was our ideal partner. Although you can't force someone to return to you, if you feel that you were meant to be together you can try this spell to seek him out again and rekindle old passions. You never know – he might be feeling exactly the same about you!

You will need

Two pins

One white candle

A piece of paper

A pen

Matches or a lighter

What you do

Do this spell on a full moon.

The two pins represent you and
your old flame. Stick one pin into one
side of the candle and the other pin
into the opposite side. Write a
message to the one you loved, and
his name, on the piece of paper and
place this under the candle.

Light the candle and say the name
of the one you wish to be reunited
with 100 times. Allow the candle to
burn down and the pins to drop. This
signifies that your message has been
received. If you notice the flame
sparking, you should hear from him –
in the form of a letter or a phone call
– within a week. If you notice a
glowing ring as the candle burns,
your wish will be granted within
28 days.

Successful first date

We all get the jitters when we're going on a date with someone new. You know how it is: your stomach is in knots and countless times you go back to the mirror to check that you look okay. This little spell will ensure that a first date goes well and that you have a pleasant time together.

You will need

A red pen

A piece of white paper

One red rose petal

One piece of red cotton thread or ribbon

One rose incense stick

Matches or a lighter

What you do

You can do this spell any time and anywhere.

Write the name of the man you are going out on a date with in red pen on the white paper, and next to it write your own name. Place the red rose petal on top of the names and then roll the paper up into a scroll. Tie it with the red cotton thread or ribbon.

Next, light the incense stick and pass the scroll of paper through the smoke. Say the following three times:

Goddess of love
Make this date successful.
Goddess of love
Make this date one
to remember.
Thank you, so mote it be.

Your meeting should go without a hitch. After your date, bury the scroll in the ground.

Spell to make him interested

Okay, I know I said you can't force someone to fall in love with you, but sometimes a man needs a hint that you are interested in him – remember, men are not mind-readers and they are only human after all! If you want to find out if someone is interested in you – and want to send out signals that you're interested in him, and then keep him interested – try this spell.

You will need

One piece of rose quartz

What you do

You can do this spell any time.

The night before you do this spell, sleep with the piece of rose quartz under your pillow. The following morning, hold the rose quartz in your dominant hand and close your eyes. Visualize your personality and all the good points about you being transferred to the rose quartz. Hold the quartz up in the air and imagine it sending out invisible signals to the person you are interested in.

Try to do this every day for one week, for ten minutes at a time. You should soon notice that the man you like has become interested in you and is beginning to look at you in a different way. You might even find that the magick has rubbed off on others, too!

A flirtation spell

We all have hang-ups that impair our self-esteem, and flirting with someone requires a certain degree of self-confidence. This little spell will boost your flirtation skills and make you feel more confident with the opposite sex.

You will need

One red candle

One pink candle

Matches or a lighter

A pinch of cinnamon

One daisy chain

What you do

Do this spell prior to going out for the evening.

Light your candles, then run yourself a warm bath. Place the pinch of cinnamon in the bath with the daisy chain that you have made. Relax in the bath and visualize how confident you will be when you go out, and how your confidence will attract men from all over the place. You will be a man-magnet tonight!

When you feel ready to do so, get out of the bath and get changed. Remember to blow out the candles. Fish the daisy chain out of the water and gently towel it dry, then place it in your handbag and take it out with you.

This is a very fast-working spell, and you should notice how quickly and easily you can flirt with a man you like, and how readily you attract men to you on your night out.

Silver moon spell

This lovely spell requires the power of the full moon. It is designed to enable you to send out romantic signals to all those wonderful, kind and suitable men out there who are looking for a princess to pamper and look after.

You will need

A silver bowl

A bottle of pure water

A small mirror (small enough to fit in the bowl)

Three drops of lavender oil

Three drops of rose oil

One floating candle

Matches or a lighter

What you do

Do this spell on the first night of a full moon.

This spell should be done at midnight, when you have peace and quiet. Fill the silver bowl with the bottled water. Drop the small mirror into the bowl, so that the mirrored side faces upwards. Put the three drops of each oil into the bowl and stir the mixture with your index finger. Light the floating candle and place it in the bowl. Put the bowl in a window where it will catch the reflection of the full moon, then say the following once:

*I wish upon the moon
tonight
To bring to me
my shining knight.
Silver moon,
Silver moon,
Silver moon.*

Leave the bowl and its contents overnight. In the morning, pour the water from the bowl onto the ground outside. You will soon see how attractive you have become.

61

Mirror, mirror on the wall

Mirrors have always held powerful magick within them, but the trick is to know how to release it. This spell will release the power of magick from a mirror and send out signals to available bachelors that you are interested in a relationship.

You will need

A handful of silver glitter

A hand-held mirror

One white candle

Matches or a lighter

What you do

Do this spell on a Friday.

Perform this spell when you have a spare half-hour to yourself. Take a bath or a shower and cleanse yourself with lots of lovely bubble bath or shower lotion. Wrap yourself in a towel, dry your hair and apply your make-up, as if you were going out on a big date. When you feel happy with the way you look, sprinkle the silver glitter all over the glass of the mirror, then light the white candle and place it in front of the mirror. Say the following words three times:

By the strike
of three
Let them see me
And bring love rushing
to me.

Blow the glitter from the mirror and look into it for a moment. See how vibrant you are! Close your eyes and count to three. By now your message will have been sent out to the universe.

Lots more men out there

They say there are 'plenty more fish in the sea' – and yes, there are, masses of them. But it's still tough when the man you thought as 'the one' turns out to be far from it. Getting over a break-up is hard to do, but this spell will remind you that there are plenty more suitable fish out there, just waiting to bite.

You will need

One red candle

Matches or a lighter

One red rose

A handful of silver glitter

A handful of gold glitter

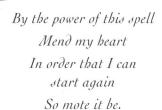

What you do

Do this spell on a full moon.

Light the red candle and place your rose and the two handfuls of glitter in front of it. Look into the flame and imagine your heartache being burned away. Now hold the rose in your hand and imagine new love entering your life and blossoming – just as a rose does. Feel the warmth from the candle flame and imagine that it's the sun entering your life once again.

Do this for as long as you feel necessary. Allow the candle to burn down, then place the silver and gold glitter in your more dominant hand and carefully take it outside. Look up to the moon and say:

By the power of this spell
Mend my heart
In order that I can
start again
So mote it be.

Blow the glitter to the moon and let her take care of the rest.

65

Lucky-in-love charm

This little charm will make sure you are always lucky in the love department. You can make it if you're in a relationship, or if you're just looking – either way, it will ensure that you won't be disappointed in your choice of partner.

You will need

One small matchbox

A handful of silver glitter

One teaspoon of mixed herbs

Scissors

One sheet of red giftwrap

A small piece of red ribbon

One red candle

Matches or a lighter

What you do

You should make this charm on a
Friday evening.

First of all, open the matchbox
and fill it with some silver glitter
and the mixed herbs. Close the
matchbox, then cut a piece of the
red paper big enough to completely
cover it. Carefully wrap the
matchbox up as if you were
wrapping a tiny present.

Take the red ribbon and tie
it round the present you've just
made. Light the red candle
and say the following words
once only:

Lucky-in-love charm
come alive
Shine on me in all matters
of the heart
So mote it be.

Wait until the candle has almost
burned down, then pour a few
drops of red candle wax onto
the parcel to seal your spell.
Carry it in your bag to attract
good luck in love to you.

Ronnie, the Rosemary Man

This is a lovely little spell for anyone who is looking for their
Mr Right, but who keeps picking Mr Wrongs. Using the
protective power of magick, this spell will ensure that only
Mr Suitables apply.

You will need

Three long sprigs of rosemary

Some cotton thread

A small circle of paper

A red pen

Some sticky tape

A small heart shape of paper

What you do

Do this spell on a waxing moon.

We don't always have an older brother to vet those who are suitable for us, so you are going to make one yourself: Ronnie will soon get to work and sort out the unscrupulous rogues from the Mr Rights!

In order to bring Ronnie alive, you need to make him: take one long sprig of rosemary and fold the top over, so that it makes a circle shape for a head. Tie it in place with some cotton thread. Now make a pair of arms and a pair of legs with the other two sprigs, tying them as before. On the circle of paper, draw a happy face, then stick the paper to the circle head you made earlier. Stick the heart-shaped paper where Ronnie's heart should be. There – finished!

Now place Ronnie on your bedroom windowsill, so that he faces out of the window. You need worry no more about attracting the wrong man – Ronnie will make sure that you don't!

When the going gets tough, the tough get spell casting!

This section of the book deals with problems concerning matters of the heart. Banishing spells should be done when the moon is waning (C-shaped moon).

People new to magick tend to think they can pay someone back by performing a hex or placing a curse on the person who has hurt them. A word of warning: please don't try to do this. Sticking a few pins into a voodoo doll or casting a spell on an ex-partner for revenge will only rebound on you – at least three times. If someone hurts you intentionally, he or she will get 'paid back' at some point in their lives by the universe. This applies to everything, and not just rotten lovers. So be satisfied with that.

Never, ever deliberately try to harm another person. That is not what magick is about. If you ever come across a book that endorses curses or negative magick, don't even bother to pick it up – it's dangerous and very harmful.

There are no spells or information in this book that can harm anyone. The aim of this section is to protect you from people who have hurt you, or to banish someone from your life. This does not mean that anything bad will happen to them; it simply means you will build up a protective barrier within you, so that this person won't bother you any more.

Stop arguments

Arguments never solve anything – all they do is sap your energy. This spell will put a halt to an argumentative partner and restore a happy, harmonious atmosphere for you both.

You will need

One onion

A knife

One blue candle

Matches or a lighter

One white candle

One white feather

What you do

Do this spell on a Saturday night when the moon is waning.

Chop the onion into four equal sections, then place one quarter in each corner of your family room. Light the blue candle and say three times:

Banish the arguments now
Banish the hostility now
Banish the hurt now
So mote it be.

Allow the blue candle to burn right down and bury any remaining wax in your garden. Wait for one hour, then light the white candle and

place the white feather next to it. Say three times:

Bring peace and
harmony now
Bring love and
excitement now
Bring happiness now
So mote it be.

Blow your wish carefully into the white feather. Allow the candle to burn down.

Take the feather outside and throw it up into the air, allowing it to be carried off into the universe. Keep the onion quarters in your home for 14 days.

Just good friends

If a man friend just won't take the hint that you aren't romantically interested in him, try this spell to make him see that you want to be just good friends and nothing more.

You will need

Something personal to him (such as a photograph, a gift, an item of jewellery or clothing)

Something personal to you

One white tea-light

Matches or a lighter

One jasmine incense stick

What you do

Do this spell on a waning moon.

Place the personal items in front of the white tea-light. Light it, and then light the incense stick using the flame of the tea-light. Wave the incense stick over both lots of personal items and say the following:

Allow the candle to burn down, then return the personal items to their rightful places. You should soon notice that your friend realizes you are not romantically interested in him, but will always be there for him.

I know that you love me
And I love you too
But not in the way you
want me to.
Let us not spoil what we
have now
And remain just good
friends for evermore.

75

To break up an affair

If you are sure that your partner is having an affair and you want to bring it to an end, try this candle spell to put a stop to it. Please remember: you cannot force anyone to do anything they don't wish to do. But if you genuinely feel this is just a phase, or a way of paying you back, then give this spell a go.

You will need

Two slips of paper

A black pen

Two silver pins

One long black candle

A heatproof plate or dish

Matches or a lighter

What you do

Do this spell on a new (dark) moon.

First of all, write the name of your partner on one slip of paper and the name of the other woman in his life on the other slip of paper, using black ink. Take a silver pin and push it through the piece of paper with his name on, then stick the pin into the candle, somewhere near the top. Take the second silver pin and stick it through the piece of paper with the woman's name on, then stick the pin into the candle, just below your partner's name.

Secure the black candle to the heatproof plate or dish, then light the candle and say:

By the power of the flame
May you return to where
you belong
I banish [name of other
woman] from our life
So that we may be as
one again
So mote it be.

Soon your partner should return to you. If he doesn't, then he is not the one for you any longer.

Recapturing first love

Romance in long-term partnerships often has to take second place, particularly if we have children to look after. This spell will recapture those special moments when you first fell in love with your partner – look out for the fireworks!

You will need

A piece of paper

A red pen

A sample of your partner's handwriting
  (such as an old love letter)

One red candle

Matches or a lighter

What you do

Do this spell on a Friday night.

Write on the piece of paper all the things that made you fall in love with your partner in the first place. Think about the first time he chatted you up. Remember how your stomach turned over whenever you saw him or heard his voice? Then write down all you can remember about what first attracted him to you.

When you've finished, place the sample of your partner's handwriting face down on your piece of paper, so that the two lots of handwriting are pressed against each other. Put the red candle on top of the two pieces of paper and light it. Say the following once:

Venus, goddess of love
Send your magick to
restore our love
Make us as we once were.
I send this message to
you above
So mote it be.

Blow out the candle and relight it for the next seven nights. You should notice that your relationship with your partner becomes as magickal as it was when you first met.

Back off, baby!

Some people just can't take 'No' for an answer, can they? This spell is designed to stop someone pestering you, when a subtle hint doesn't work.

You will need

One teaspoon of sea salt

One dark blue candle

Matches or a lighter

Two drops of lavender oil

A hair from the person who is bothering you
(or a sample of writing, see right)

A heatproof dish

What you do

Do this spell on a waning moon, and on a Saturday if possible.

You can obtain a hair from the person in question from his hairbrush – failing that, try to get a sample of his signature or at least a sample of his handwriting.

Cast a circle of salt round the blue candle – this will protect you. Light the candle, then rub the lavender oil onto the palms of your hands – this will also protect you from any negative reactions. Take the sample of hair or handwriting and set it alight in the flame from the candle. Allow it to burn completely by dropping it into the heatproof dish. Say the following three times:

[Name of person] be gone from my life
It is now time to move on
And let me do the same.
You will be out of my life from this day forth
And never bother me again.

Allow the candle to burn right down and throw any remaining wax right away from your home.

You should only do this spell if you really don't want the other person ever to bother you again.

Prejudice spell

Not all relationships are heterosexual, and relationship magick isn't exclusively for couples of the opposite sex. This spell is specifically designed to stop the prejudices that other couples may encounter on a daily basis. True, you are never going to please everyone, and there will always be some people who think your relationship is wrong. But this spell will keep you protected, and will stop people who feel this way from hurting you.

You will need

One black candle

One pin

Matches or a lighter

What you do

Do this spell on a waning moon.

Think for a moment of the times where you've come across prejudice in your relationship with your partner. Push the pin through the candle, halfway down. Light the candle. While the first half of it burns down, you will be sending out invisible messages to all those who are against you and your partner. As the candle melts, the pin will drop – leave it to merge with the melted wax. The second half of the candle will banish those ignorant people from your life, and allow you to live as you choose with the person of your choice.

Once the candle has burned right down, scrape up the wax and the pin and pop them into a freezer bag. As you place this in your freezer, say the following:

No longer will we be under attack
From this day forth we will be free to live out our lives as we wish.
People who don't approve will be frozen out of our lives And no longer bother us
So mote it be.

West Side Story spell

It's not easy trying to maintain a happy relationship when your friends and family are against it right from the start. Whether it's because you're from a different culture, colour, race or background, this spell will banish any animosity, so that you are free to date whomever you wish to.

You will need

One red candle

One blue candle

An item that represents you and your partner
(a gift of jewellery that he has given you or
a photograph of you together is ideal)

One teaspoon of mixed herbs

One teaspoon of salt

Matches or a lighter

What you do

Do this spell on a waning moon.

Place the red candle and blue candle next to each other. Put the item relating to you and your partner in front of the two candles. Place the herbs and salt on top of the item. Light the blue candle first, and say:

By the power of the
goddess of love
I hereby ask you to banish
the interference of others
From our lives
Let me be free to make my
own choices in love.

Allow the blue candle to burn down. Then light the red candle, and say:

By the power of the
goddess of love
Allow our love to conquer all
May we be happy
for evermore.

Allow the red candle to burn down. Take the herb and salt mixture and throw it out of the window. Finish the spell by saying:

This is my wish,
so mote it be.

Second chance

If you've been hurt by a loved one and genuinely think that he deserves a second chance, perform this spell to heal the hurt you've suffered and to give your man another chance.

You will need

Three strands of your partner's hair

A piece of plain paper

One dark blue candle

Matches or a lighter

One red candle

One white candle

What you do

Do this spell on a Friday night and a waxing moon.

Okay, he might deserve it, but don't go up behind your man and yank his hair out! Instead, it is better to obtain the three hairs you need from his hairbrush. Place the three strands in a row on the plain paper so that you can see them. First of all, light the dark blue candle. While it is burning, say the following once:

By the power of this flame
I banish the pain.

Take one strand of hair and burn it in the flame – being careful not to singe your fingers! Allow the blue candle to burn while you light the red candle. Say once:

By the power of this flame
our love returns again.

Take another strand of hair and burn it in the flame of the red candle. Allow the red and blue candles to continue to burn, and finally light the white candle. Say once:

By the power of this flame
peace will return.

Take the third strand of hair and burn it in the flame of the white candle. Allow all three candles to burn down safely.

I don't love you any more

Sometimes a relationship becomes stale and you know you must move on, but your partner just won't take the hint and no number of words will make him see that you don't love him any more. This spell will send the subtle hint that you should no longer be together – without hurting his feelings.

You will need

A photograph of the two of you

One black candle

Matches or a lighter

One ice-cube

One teaspoon of salt

What you do

Do this spell on a waning moon.

Take the photograph of both of you and rip it in two, so that you are now separated. This may at first seem cruel, but sometimes you have to be cruel to be kind. Light the black candle and place the part of the photograph with your partner's picture on it in front of the candle. Place the ice-cube on top of his picture, then say the following words:

This time in my life must come to an end In order to create new beginnings. The power of water melts you away And sends you on your way.

Pour the salt onto the photograph. The salt will melt the ice-cube – as well as your relationship.

To change a situation

You might at some point in your life find yourself in an intolerable situation in a relationship and want to change it so that you are happy once more. This spell will do just that and will change the situation from sad to happy.

You will need

A small black circle of paper

A pen

One black candle

One teaspoon of black pepper

Matches or a lighter

A small yellow circle of paper

One yellow candle

One teaspoon of salt

What you do

Do this spell on a new (dark) moon.

Draw a sad face on the black circle of paper and place it under the black candle. This represents the sad situation you are in right now. Sprinkle the black pepper round the black candle and then light it. Say the following:

I banish this sadness
in my life
I banish this situation
for good
As of now, so mote it be.

When the candle has burned down, draw a smiley face on the yellow circle of paper, and place it under the yellow candle. Sprinkle the salt round the candle and then light it. Say the following:

By the power of this spell
I create happy times for me
This is my wish,
so mote it be.

Allow the candle to burn down. You should see an improvement in your relationship situation very soon.

Happy parting

Sometimes we just know that a relationship isn't going to work out and it's best for all concerned to end it. Do this spell one week before you tell your partner – this should result in a happy parting for all concerned.

You will need

Queen of Hearts playing card

King of Hearts playing card

A pen

One black pebble

A fish pond or river

What you do

Do this spell on a waning moon.

Write your name on the Queen of Hearts playing card and your partner's name on the King of Hearts card. Lay the Queen of Hearts face up on a table, and place the black pebble on top of it. Now lay the King of Hearts face down on top, so as to make a kind of sandwich. Hold your more dominant hand over the sandwich and say:

For us to move on
This time must end
We will both be free
and happy
And remain for ever
friends.

Fold the two cards in two and dispose of them in a wastebin. Throw the black pebble into a fish pond or a river. Your parting should now be a smooth and happy one.

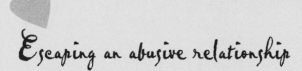

Escaping an abusive relationship

No woman should suffer at the hands of her partner – be it physical or mental abuse. If you find yourself in this position, the first thing you must do is seek help from the appropriate authorities. No, he won't change, no matter how many promises and how many times he says, 'I'm sorry, I didn't mean it.' This charm will help protect you from any further abuse, but only *you* have the power inside to break the habit.

You will need

A pinch of cardamom

A pinch of mustard powder

One teaspoon of sea salt

A small bowl

A small pill pot

One black candle

A photograph of the abuser

Matches or a lighter

A heatproof dish

What you do

You should do this spell on a full or waning moon.

Mix the spices and salt together in a small bowl, then fill the pill pot with the mixture. Place the black candle on top of the photograph and light it. As it burns down, say the following:

You will harm me no more
I have more power than you now
I will always be protected.
You cannot harm me again
This is law, so mote it be.

Set fire to the photograph and let it burn to ash in the heatproof dish. Allow the candle to burn down and then dispose of any remaining wax and ash as far away as you can. Keep the pill pot with you at all times.

Getting out of a situation you now regret

This spell from America works well for any situation that you regret having got involved in – including your love life. It might be getting involved with a man whom you discover is married with six kids, or finding that you are dating someone completely unsuitable. You need to do this spell for nine nights for it to take full effect.

You will need

Nine white tea-lights

A piece of paper or card

A pen

Matches or a lighter

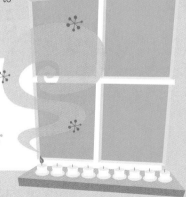

What you do

Start this spell on a Monday and a waning moon.

Place the nine tea-lights in a row on a windowsill where they won't be disturbed. Write the words of this spell down on a piece of paper or card, so that you don't have to keep referring to the book. Place it near the tea-lights, but not so close that they will catch fire. Then light the first tea-light and say the following spell-binding words:

*Foolish was I
But no more.
The light I now see
Will guide me
And release me from this situation
Thank you, so mote it be.*

Do this ritual at the same time every night for the next eight nights – you should soon be rid of the situation in which you regret becoming involved.

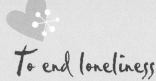

To end loneliness

It can sometimes feel as if you're the only person in the world who doesn't have a partner. Well-meaning friends invite you to dinner parties and you end up feeling like a big, fat gooseberry. This little spell, handed down to me by a very dear friend, will end your loneliness in love and will stop you from having to buy meals for one any more.

You will need

A small piece of paper

A pen

One peach

A flower pot with some soil in it

What you do

You should do this spell on a full or new (dark) moon.

Write down the following on the piece of paper:

*This spell will end my
loneliness*

*Like this peach, my life will
be sweet with opportunity*

As this grows, so will I grow

*Bringing an end to
my loneliness*

So mote it be.

Eat the peach and taste how sweet your life is going to be. Enjoy the sumptuous fruit and, when you've finished it, keep the stone from the centre. Wrap the peach stone in the piece of paper and bury it in the flower pot.

As the paper degrades, so will your loneliness. As a new peach begins to grow, so will the interest from potential suitors. You might even grow a peach tree!

99

A make-it-better box

This is a lovely little charm to make the heartache go away when someone's dumped you. The items listed below are merely suggestions – you can put whatever you like in your 'first aid' box of comfort. This charm is also the ideal present for a girlfriend who always seems to find Mr Wrong!

You will need

An empty shoe box

Giftwrap paper

A handful of dried lavender

A few luxury chocolates

One small bottle of bubble bath

One small bottle of champagne

One new lipstick

One small teddy bear

One comedy DVD film

One pair of fluffy socks

A length of red ribbon

What you do

You can do this spell any time and anywhere.

First of all, cover the shoe box (including the lid) with some pretty giftwrap. Layer the bottom of the box with the dried lavender – this not only has healing properties, but will make the box smell delicious.

Now place all your chosen items inside the box and tie it up with a big red ribbon.

Whenever you feel in need of a bit of loving first aid, have a relaxing bath, put your fluffy socks on and use all the items in the box to cheer yourself up. It works every time!

Decisions, decisions!

Sometimes you might find yourself torn between two men and wonder which one will make you happier. One might lavish you with expensive gifts, while the other takes you for romantic walks in the moonlight and recites poetry to you. Use this spell to help you make a decision.

You will need

Jack of Diamonds playing card
Jack of Hearts playing card
Two red rose petals
Six drops of rose oil
One white tea-light
Matches or a lighter

What you do

Do this spell on a Friday and a full or new (dark) moon.

Take the Jack of Diamonds and the Jack of Hearts and decide which card is going to represent which man in your life. Place one rose petal on top of each card. Now put three drops of rose oil onto each card and light the white tea-light. Close your eyes and say the following words:

Goddess of love,
I need your help
To help me to make up
my mind.
May you be judge and jury
And decide who is best
for me
Thank you, so mote it be.

Allow the tea-light to burn down. Soon you will know which of your two interested suitors you should choose. The answer often comes in a dream.

Stay, don't stray

Are you suspicious that your partner might have a roving eye? It's an awful feeling to think that he might be betraying you. This spell will ensure that he doesn't even think about doing the dirty on you.

You will need

One small Spanish onion

A knife

Two blue cornflowers

A pinch of pepper

A blue handkerchief

What you do

Do this spell on a Saturday night and a full moon.

Cut the onion into four pieces and place them, the cornflowers and the pinch of pepper in the centre of the handkerchief. Hold your hands over the open handkerchief and say the following words:

[Name of partner], you will never stray from me
And you will never betray me.
Blue is the colour of banish
And my worries have now gone.

Fold the four corners of the handkerchief into the centre and tie them in a big knot at the top. Place the package on a windowsill that will catch the moonlight for one night. The following day place the package under the bed you share, or under your own bed, until the next full moon in about 28 days' time.

Banish the green-eyed monster

Jealousy does nothing but destroy a relationship, but some men just can't help themselves and become possessive and suspicious of your every move. If you're having problems with a jealous partner, try the green-eyed monster spell.

You will need

A black pen

A piece of green card or letter paper

Scissors

One green candle

Matches or a lighter

A heatproof dish

What you do

Do this spell on a waning moon.

First of all, you have to symbolize your green-eyed monster by making a drawing of his face. Take the black pen and draw a huge monster face to cover the piece of card or paper. You don't have to be a great artist or even any good at drawing – make him as funny, ridiculous or monstrous as you like. Then cut the face out. Next, light the green candle and say the following:

Your jealousy is driving us apart
I banish your jealousy for evermore
Your jealousy goes out the door
This is my quest, so mote it be.
The spell is working, you will now see.

Screw the monster's face up into a ball and, using the flame of the candle, carefully set light to the paper or card in the heatproof dish. Allow the candle to burn down and your wish should be granted.

A major falling out

We can all get a bit hot-headed from time to time and say things we don't really mean. This spell will reverse the insults you and your partner have exchanged, when you've had one of those almighty rows and have maybe come out with some things you wish you hadn't. If saying sorry doesn't cut it, try this reversal spell instead.

You will need

A handful of salt

A small hand-held mirror

What you do

Do this spell on a new (dark) moon.

First of all, find an area where you can sit undisturbed for ten minutes. Cast a circle of salt round you and the mirror. Look into the mirror and try to look past your own reflection. Your eyes might glaze over and water, but don't worry – you know you're doing it correctly if this happens. Say the following:

Mirror, mirror, in my hand
Please listen to my command
By the power of thoughts inside my head
Take back all the awful things we said.

Repeat this five times, then turn the mirror so that you can no longer see yourself in it. The reversal spell is now complete, and you and your partner will never again refer to the falling out.

Mend your ways

All relationships have their ups and downs, and after a while of being together we often feel as though we're being taken for granted by our partner. This spell will help you to mend his ways and ensure that he turns back into the charming man you used to know and starts treating you like a princess again. The sugar and honey will add sweetness to your life, the ginger and mixed spice will pep up your love life, and the oak leaf will carry your desire across the universe.

You will need

One teaspoon of sugar

One teaspoon of mixed spice

One teaspoon of ground ginger

A mixing bowl

One teaspoon of honey

A wooden spoon

One oak leaf

A river or stream

What you do

You can do this spell on any day and at any time of the month.

Mix the sugar, mixed spice and ginger together in a bowl, then pour the honey over the mixture. Stir with a wooden spoon until you have a thick pastelike substance. Take the oak leaf and smear the mixture all over the leaf.

Now take your oak leaf and stand either on a bridge or on the bank of a river or stream. Say the following:

Body of water, take my wish to the universe
Grant me that [name of partner] will mend his ways
And treat me how I deserve to be treated
So mote it be.

Close your eyes and count backwards from ten to one, then throw the oak leaf into the river or stream. Leave and don't look back.

111

Please call me

You've met the most wonderful, kind and caring guy, had a marvellous first date – now what? Should you call him first? Should he make the first move and call you? If you've just met someone who you think might be Mr Right, don't sit by the phone all day. Instead, perform a little bit of practical magick with this easy-to-follow spell!

You will need

A pink pen

A small piece of pink paper

A phone

What you do

You can do this spell any time and anywhere.

Take the coloured pen and piece of pink paper and draw a big heart in the centre. Within the heart write your man's name five times and draw a picture of him. It doesn't matter if you're not artistic – a stickman will do. Underneath your picture, and still within the heart, write the words 'Please call me'. Place the paper under your phone and say the following words:

Goddess Venus, send this message to [name of the man in question] To call me Thank you, so mote it be.

You should hear from the man you're interested in within a week. Remember to make sure you've given him your phone number! If you don't hear from him within one week, do the spell again.

When three's a crowd

A relationship should consist of two people – not three, four or more. If your man can't make his mind up about who he wants to be with, this little spell will help sort out the situation.

You will need

A piece of black card or letter paper, folded in half

A gold or silver pen

One envelope

One black candle

Matches or a lighter

What you do

Do this spell on a Saturday or a waning moon.

Take the piece of card or paper and write down the following words in gold or silver ink:

The time has come for you to make up your mind
This letter will do this for you.
You are no longer allowed to play with other people's feelings in this way
I send this message to the universe.

Place the letter in the envelope and put it under the black candle. Light the candle and, when it has burned down halfway, set fire to the envelope in the flame of the candle and throw the envelope quickly outdoors – be very careful not to burn your fingers!

Allow the candle to burn right down and throw any remaining wax out of the door, too. This should get your man to make his mind up.

Interfering in-laws

Yes, I know they're only trying to be well-meaning, but when in-laws are interfering so much that it is spoiling your relationship, it's time to call on a little bit of magick to help you out. This spell, originally designed by a friend of mine, won't harm anyone – it will just enter the subconscious, so that the in-law in question will interfere no more.

You will need

A photograph of the interfering in-law

One blue candle

Matches or a lighter

One blue balloon

One blue feather

One teaspoon of black pepper

What you do

Do this spell on a waning moon.

Place the photograph of the in-law who is interfering in your love life behind the blue candle, then light the candle. Blow the balloon up just enough so that it forms a bulb shape and carefully push the feather inside. Hold on to the neck of the balloon to keep the air inside, then carefully pinch the black pepper between your fingertips and push it into the balloon. This might seem a little tricky at first, but you will manage it in the end. Don't worry if all the pepper doesn't go in.

Blow the balloon up so that it is full of air and tie a knot at the end. Say the following three times:

By the element of the air
Carry this message to
[name of in-law]
So that he/she will no
longer interfere
And we will be free to lead
our own lives
This is my message,
so mote it be.

Allow the candle to burn down and then release the balloon into the sky. The in-law should stop interfering, but if this spell doesn't work, repeat it in 28 days' time.

117

Divorce spell

Sometimes it's kinder to everyone involved to dissolve the marriage and to divorce. A separation of any kind doesn't have to result in a war of spiteful words and name-calling. Nor does it have to involve hurting other people. If you've tried reconciliation and decided that divorce is the only option, think of it as a celebration and as a change for the better. This spell will ensure that all runs smoothly.

You will need

A photocopy of your marriage certificate

One thin pink candle

Your wedding ring

His wedding ring

Matches or a lighter

What you do

Do this spell on a new (dark) moon.

Place the photocopy of your
marriage certificate under the
pink candle. Next, place both
wedding rings over the top of the
candle. Light the candle and say
the following:

*The good times were good,
the bad times were bad
Although we will part, we
won't be sad
The time has come to
now move on
All our troubles
will now be gone.*

*May we stay friends
for evermore
Now is the time to close
the door.*

As the candle burns down, the
rings will drop onto the copy of the
marriage certificate. Fold the
certificate in four and pour a few
drops of wax on to it to seal it. Bury
it in the garden where the family
home is. Keep the wedding rings,
as these will ensure that there are
no ill feelings.

Stop hurting me

Being hurt over and over again is just not funny. It knocks your confidence and destroys your self-esteem. If your partner takes pleasure from mentally hurting you, put a stop to it now by doing this simple letter spell. You won't actually send the letter, but it will have the same effect as if you delivered it to him yourself!

You will need

One black candle

Matches or a lighter

A sheet or two of writing paper

A black pen

A heatproof dish

What you do

Do this spell on a waning moon.

Light the black candle to begin the process of banishing your pain. Sit comfortably and think about all the things your partner has done to hurt you. It might be harsh words that he's said to you; belittling you in public; staying out in bars for all hours of the night; or leaving you at home while he goes off womanizing – anything and everything you feel has been hurtful to you, write it down. Don't be shy, for no one is ever going to read this letter.

When you feel as though you've got everything out of your system, fold the paper in three and say the following:

I banish the pain you've caused me in my heart
I banish any more hurt henceforth.
I will not allow you to hurt me any more
So mote it be.

Place the paper in the candle flame and burn it in the heatproof dish – being careful not to burn your fingers. The universe will send this silent message to your partner, and your relationship should improve.

121

Please be friends

Sometimes your friends won't immediately take to the new man in your life, and you may be torn between being faithful to your girlfriends and being faithful to your partner. If your friends hate your boyfriend, and keep telling you he's no good for you and is taking up too much of your time, try this spell to regain peace and quiet in your life – the charm is going to be your personal peace bracelet.

You will need

Some vanilla oil or essence

A small bowl

Some small wooden beads

A sheet of paper towel

A thin piece of elastic

What you do

Do this spell on a new (dark) moon.

First of all, place the vanilla oil or essence in a bowl and drop the wooden beads into it. Cover each bead with the oil, then place them on a paper towel to dry out.

Take the elastic and measure round your wrist. Cut it to the length you need to make a bracelet and tie a secure knot at one end. One by one, place the beads on the elastic and, as you do so, repeat the following words with each bead:

When you have a full row of beads, tie the elastic securely and wear the peace bracelet whenever you are with your friends or partner. Your friends will soon accept your new man.

*Peace and goodwill to
all I know.*

123

Conclusion

We have now come to the end of this little cauldron of love spells and I hope I have covered every eventuality in matters of the heart. If you are in a situation that I haven't touched upon, don't worry, for you can easily design your own spell by following the simple steps below. Self-made spells work more quickly than pre-designed spells because they come straight from the heart.

• If you wish to bring love into your life, perform your spell on a new (dark) moon, a full moon or a waxing moon – see the moon phases on page 12.

• If you wish to banish someone from your life, or banish a situation in your love life, then perform your spell on a new or waning moon.

• For increasing love, use a pink or a red candle.

• For decreasing and banishing love, use a blue or a black candle.

- Decide on what you want your spell to achieve and try to put it into simple words. It helps if you write it down, so that if you need to use the spell again, you have it to hand.

- Visualize what it is that you want to achieve so that it becomes real in your mind.

- If you want to enhance your spells, call on nature to lend a hand. Rose petals, buttercups, daisies, cornflowers and leaves from strong trees (such as the oak) all help in matters of the heart.

- Allow your spell to run for 28 days before you try it again, and remember that the goddess of love can work in mysterious ways, which you might not expect.

- If you do a spell and then regret doing it, simply retract it by placing a small mirror in front of a black candle. Light the candle and stare straight through the flame. Say five times, 'Spell, retract'. Allow the candle to burn down. Your spell will then be retracted and you need not worry any more.

I hope you have enjoyed reading this book. Whenever you have a problem in your love life, pick it up and you will find the answer.

Index

Executive Editor *Brenda Rosen*
Managing Editor *Clare Churly*
Executive Art Editor *Sally Bond*
Designer *Pia Hietarinta for Cobalt id*
Illustrator *Arlene Adams*
Senior Production Controller *Ian Paton*